SISTER
ZERO

Other Books By Nance Van Winckel

VISUAL POETRY

Book of No Ledge (Pleiades Press, 2016)

POETRY

The Many Beds of Martha Washington (The Pacific Northwest Poetry Series, Lynx House Press, 2021)
Our Foreigner (Beyond Baroque Books, 2017)
Pacific Walkers (University of Washington Press, 2013)
No Starling (University of Washington Press, 2007)
Beside Ourselves (Miami University Press, 2003)
After a Spell (Miami University Press, 1998)
A Measure of Heaven (Floating Bridge Press, 1996)
The Dirt (Miami University Press, 1996)
Bad Girl, With Hawk (University of Illinois Press, 1987)
The 24 Doors: Advent Calendar Poems (Bieler Press, 1985)

FICTION

Ever Yrs (Twisted Road Publications, 2014)
Boneland (University of Oklahoma Press, 2013)
Curtain Creek Farm (Persea Books, 2001)
Limited Lifetime Warranty (University of Missouri Press, 1997)

NANCE VAN WINCKEL

SISTER ZERO

A MEMOIR

SLANT
BOOKS

SISTER ZERO
A Memoir

Slant Books
P.O. Box 60295
Seattle, WA 98160

www.slantbooks.com

HARDCOVER ISBN: 978-1-63982-118-1
PAPERBACK ISBN: 978-1-63982-117-4
EBOOK ISBN: 978-1-63982-119-8

Cataloguing-in-Publication data:

Names: Van Winckel, Nance.

Title: Sister Zero: A Memoir / Nance Van Winckel.

Description: Seattle, WA: Slant Books, 2022.

Identifiers: ISBN 978-1-63982-118-1 (hardcover) |ISBN 978-1-63982-117-4 (paperback) |
    ISBN 978-1-63982-119-8 (ebook)

Subjects: LCSH: Sisters. | Loss (Psychology). | Bereavement -- Family relationships. |
    Grief -- Family relationships.

Classification: PS3572.A546 S57 2022 (paperback) | PS3572.A546 S57 2022 (ebook)

For my nephew Cameron,
my mother Mary Lee,
and my sister Sarah.

And he said unto them, *Take me up, and cast me forth into the sea; so shall the sea be calm unto you: for I know that for my sake this great tempest is upon you.*

—*Jonah* 1:12

CONTENTS

I. Close Your Eyes | 1

II. Follow the Smoke Rings | 13

III. Nothing Here Will Come to Pass | 23

IV. Couched in an Era | 35

V. Where Your Hideous Rainbow Ends | 47

VI. Autopsy Report in Progressland | 59

VII. Doomsday Neareth | 71

VIII. The Equitable Life | 81

IX. Time Capsule Components | 93

X. Little Hope, Little Sarah Belle | 103

XI. High Upstairs | 113

XII. The Vast Maybe | 127

Acknowledgments | 143

AWAITING DEVELOPMENTS, AT THE 1964 NEW YORK WORLD'S FAIR

My family waits for the Polaroid to dry. It takes its time. Finger by finger, my sister pulls off her gloves. The next Just War puts on its boots. Illness circling, and nobody materializing here before our eyes sees well enough to recognize a seeping sore.

Slowly we eventuate, then hand ourselves around. We've admired the backdrop of our planet as a silver fountain. But this planet's drenched! Sparkling! Beautifully contained!

Then "*whoops!*" shouts a worker whose auger has suddenly disappeared down a pipe and into a hole. "All she wrote," he says as my family stares down, then bends down, ears tipped to the tool's grinding on: its tightening, its turning.

I STEP OFF, LATE

Years later my sister was a nurse. Dying, the last thing she'd done was check her own pulse. Two fingers on her neck. The gumption to do that, or write this: *Just. Press. Harder.*

Which was how her hand stayed, hours later, even in the black bag zipped up on the gurney going out.

I catch the last train of the week. It slips into a tunnel and comes out on a lake ringed by birches. I step off, late, carrying black shoes. The animals are all racing to get behind me—deer, dogs, ponies—ears pressed back against their skulls.

No matter how fast I run, I doubt I can hurdle that fence, though a scrap from a girl's dress flaps there on a post. *So,* I keep thinking, so it *is* possible.

NECK OF THE WOODS

Driving through my sister's old neighborhood, I turn right, left, right, never quite sure which had been her house, or even her street.

Somewhere around here.

Here, where I live now and she lived then.

A gone-too-longness presses down with the weight of a squat grey house fringed by bishop's weed. Was *that* the one? Although filled with strangers, many houses seem familiar.

Then, when she was last alive, I had gone only once to her house. I'd brought a woven basket for her new baby, lined it, and sewn blue ribbons into it, adding at the last a few glittery glass beads to its rim. These my sister immediately cut loose, saying nothing, just shaking her head and rolling her eyes in my general direction.

I turn back. The weeds wink. And now, like then—how loudly her scissors snip the knots.

FROM WHATEVER HOUSE HAD BEEN MY SISTER'S

I took her baby home with me. In the silly basket I'd given her.

Because he was too much. Because her leg was in a cast and she couldn't very well carry him and herself up the steep stairway, now could she? Because he was crying right then, and so was she, and because she asked me to, and because it was one thing, one thing, one thing I could do for her.

> What does he eat? What
> does he drink? How
> much and how often?

She handed me a bottle and a box of formula. I was told to *read* the directions. "Read the back." (Pointing.) "Read all of this right here."

I was told the baby would tell me when and how much. "And Christ, you better believe he'll tell you."

LANDERLUNDEN

Anywhere I go in America, my mother's been there too, or so she says. Lived there. Vacationed there. Even a city I make up: Landerlunden. "Oh yes, it was full of lilacs. You girls rode your bikes around a park there." And on she goes until slowly it slides into my view too. Was there a forest encircling it? "Yes, and those foxes and their tracks we followed out from town, us carrying those awful pistols, and what a racket in the trees when the hounds flushed the pretty red one. Honey, I want you to have the stole we made from him. Remember it? His mouth is a little clip that opens and closes like this: {here her hand becomes a snout, biting}."

HER LIFE

My sister didn't have a boyfriend but she'd picked someone out. A married man. A jerk, she'd said, but who cares.

The jerk had no idea what was coming. He'd demanded a paternity test, but the baby was indeed his, and the court made him pay.

And the baby. Soon he's crawling. He spits yellow goo on the green shag carpet, and my sister says, "I quit, I give up, uncle."

I watch her inhale then blow a perfect smoke ring the baby slips his fist through.

Her plan in her mind. I'd been told to just listen. She'd said she wanted to leave something of herself behind since how long did she really have anyway and a baby would bring joy to her pathetic life. Said she had it all figured out. Said I should shut up and support her and not argue with every friggin' thing she said. So what if it was a huge mistake? It was hers to make. Her life. And she could screw it up any way she wanted. Said she was tired and depressed and mentioned again that bit about the baby and the joy.

THE BABY

The baby got big and banged holes in the walls. Fist-sized. The baby got a heavy coat for Xmas and stormed out into a snowy night, telling us all to Get Real, to Go to Hell, to Eat Shit.

The baby pocketed my friends' children's ninjas. The baby got shipped around to A) a father, B) an aunt, C) a grandmother, & back to A, then to C, & B again, & so on.

The baby hated school and loved Jimi Hendrix. Loathed any vegetable, loved all drugs. The baby's teeth went bad; his eyes went bad & then went yellow. He robbed and lied and went to jail.

The baby was a dead man at 24. The large weight of his small urn surprised me. I couldn't look at it. The baby was in there. I'd been the one to name him. ("Ask *her*," my sister'd said to a nurse. "She's got a bazillion words.")

I stare at the baby's name in the stone and kick snow off the letters. It blows right back. My mother says she sort of remembers the baby. "Wasn't he quite fussy?" She squints into the wind, trying . . . trying. Says she's sure she'll remember the later him later.

FAULT VS. VAULT

My sister's eleven when she gets the first diagnosis: juvenile rheuma-toid arthritis. My mother's lip quivers when she tells me. I'm 16. I'm her other problem. Since I'm often up to no good with boys and gin fizz and motorcycles, I have a probation officer. Plus, lately I'm failing P.E. because I cannot, will not, no way in hell, leap over the goddamn horse.

Listening to my mother's news, my first thought is, my fault. I drift back.

Back. Seeing in my mind's eye my seven-year-old self pushing my two-year-old sister on her trike. Faster, peddle fast! I push harder. Then she's crying. What a baby, I taunt her—so sure she's crying because I'm pushing too fast.

But no, she's crying because I've broken her leg. It's stuck in the trike's spokes.

Two dark months later, I step over the toddler who's on her butt, loudly dragging her bright white cast across the kitchen floor.

I'm sorry. Sorry, sorry. I'm crying. "It's not your fault, honey." My mother takes my hands. "Not yours."

Cry baby, why worry the sorry, worry the fault rising fast in the won-dering loitering here, where who, anyway, will ever believe what the mother just said?

MISTER ED ADORED FDR

Mister Ed quotes Roosevelt, a man, Ed says, who never feared fear, which is what Ed says he mainly fears. Fear.

I look out the window. I'm a kid. I sense that fearing fear is an *idea*. Ideas require thought. Thought requires space. I blink into a snowflake.

Then Carol shouts at Wilbur. "But we only kept Ed because he came with the house! Ed should be *locked up!*"

Locked up = fear = fear of fear. The deepest fears loom highest. What doesn't Carol get?

Ed says his ears have been burning and if he were a cat he'd be up a tree. Then he phones the SPCA and asks for the Cruelty to Horses Department. "What I really *need*—and make it snappy!—is a carrot pizza."

Carrots! Pizza! These are not ideas. Snow out a window. Snow in the TV's box. Flakes fly. What I feared fearing: that the more frightened I was, the more frightening I became.

Ed says women are beyond comprehension. His ears flap—two exclamations!! "Wilbur, it's useless to even try to understand. It's bigger than the both of us!"

Wind inside, and wind out. Snow in the room's silence, chaos in impenetrable gusts, and Ed snaps back at the nothingness: "All I want behind myself is my tail."

Meet me under the smoke rings . . . at General Cigar's Hall of Ruins.

Turn at the corner of mouth and mole. Proceed
along the dream skin. Doesn't the route seem
self-explanatory? Knock at each temple: ruin, ruin.
    The answer resounds in stereo.

—HOW DO YOU GET THERE?
JUST FOLLOW THE SMOKE RINGS!

MONITORS OF THE GUEST BOOK

My mother's bank-teller friends suggested she put a white lace hankie and a rose in my sister's clasped hands. Her boy, ten, rolled his eyes. Then I did. When he'd hidden her cigarette lighter in the casket with her, I'd nodded. Now we sat outside the viewing room like two bugs among the flowers. He kept asking for the pen back after someone signed in and walked off with it. Such was his job. Behind us: the melodramatic ahs and oohs over that droopy rose. The boy sighed. I shook my head. He rolled his eyes.

BIG O'S

I spot her gold coat first, and then *her*. Her bundled in it on the sidewalk. By Big-O Tires. The traffic light stirs red whirlwinds on the street where my car and I sit behind *stop*.

And although she's been dead for a month, my sister crosses the intersection.

I jerk wider awake, watching the gilt streak of her.

She passes the tire workers who lean and smoke against a stack of O's. And no doubt an O is the shape of my mouth as I stare. Then the huge yellow coat turns, and yes, but for the two black teeth, she could almost *be* my sister.

I roll down my window and call her name into the traffic, where such sounds are battered, bleeped over, and roundly splattered . . . and thus incapable of reaching the woman hurrying towards the Plasma Center, where a guard has just opened the doors to the donors, who crowd forward, a gold figure in their midst.

OBVIOUSLY:
PANHANDLER BY THE FREEWAY

"Shoot me if I ever get like that," my sister said one day. I was driving her somewhere.

Well, don't get like that, I said.

"Everyone's just flipping that guy off. Sheesh."

Don't.

"I won't."

Panhandler. Obviously when I told my sister about (obviously) the word's etymology—to handle a beggar's pan—when I looked obviously over, she was, obviously, asleep.

Shoot me for saying I don't or won't or can't stop saying shoot.

Twenty-five years later: same spot, another guy. Only it's this one's dog that wears the sign: *Evey nikel heps*.

She didn't, I mouth to the man, which makes his dog woof and the light change and the driver behind me honk twice and flip me off.

Don't, someone said.

I won't, someone answered.

HOME WITH ME

Since of course there's no crib, a friend suggests I keep my sister's baby in an open suitcase. So there he is. At home on my office floor. I'm trying to read my students' stories, and he's shrieking. He stops when I lift him and coo to him, but as soon as I bundle him back into the suitcase, he picks right up where he left off. *Sorry, baby*, I say. *I have to work. Sorry, baby, I don't know what's wrong with you.*

Sleep-deprived. Behind in my grading. While I'm in class a bevy of student babysitters drifts in and out of my office/nursery. *I'm sorry, baby*, I say when I get home and stare into his red swollen eyes. The scrunched face utters renewed wails. I have no idea what I'm doing. Why won't he calm down? I'm failing the baby. Why won't he sleep? I'm failing everything.

At my doctor's office I shout over the baby's wails. I explain about the narcotics my sister was taking while she was pregnant. Since I looked. In her purse. Percocets. Oxy-something. And the smoking. The doctor nods and runs her hand over the baby's cheek. "Well, that's the answer then," she says. "He's in withdrawal."

When I start sobbing the baby peers up at me, his eyes the same amber as my sister's, and—for just a moment—my tears stop his.

TRYING TO BRING YOU UP
TO SPEED

So here's the thing. Lately I have to help Mom get dressed so you might as well help too since you're quasi-here and I'm jabbering away at you. You can call her Buba. She likes it now. I don't know, Hebrew maybe? Let's put this shirt in the wash; she's been wearing it all week. What the hell is going on indeed. You can't hardly get it off her—"Buba, lift your arms"—see, that makes her smile. Try it. Say it. I don't care how far gone you are, you always were, and anyhow, Far Gone is now her middle name.

WHAT THE HELL INDEED

Tell your dead self you're sorry, I wordlessly tell my deceased sister at the funeral parlor, where the attendant had just shown me The *Dress.* On *Her.*

Can you see yourself? Dead, I mean? You look awful. I continue silently scolding her as she's closed up and wheeled back into the cold. *See. There's our mother running her hand along those pink polyester casket pillows. No doubt she's thinking about hell. Since she's worried* that's *where you'll end up. Or already are.*

She's frantic, beside herself believing she'll never meet you again in the next where-ever. And mainly, she's upset because she's suddenly unsure of everything she used to be sure of. Okay, see, she's finally decided on that pink piece of shit pillow for your box. You deserve it. Watch her write the check now. Go on, take a last parting shot.

BINARIES

The monitor goes dark. Yikes, it's all a zero-or-one-thing, isn't it, or it won't work. It's a zero. Or it's one. What don't you get?

Except tonight you nod up to every single non-binary whatever; all are lit up in space—lit up and fucking every other non-binary whatever under this night's throbbing totemic moon. All the butts flash. Infinite colors of skin, of flesh. Flash flash and more flash.

Never just the one. Never a mere zero. Never more or less. Never richer or poorer. Never giver or taker. Sicker or well. Never a sole dot on a sole line on a graph that goes by one name.

No one comes from one. No lone shard flies between the black nothing and the flung-together all-shards of the *what* and its *ever*.

MISTER ED CLAIMS JONAH FIRST CONSIDERED SKEDADDLING

To Spain, Ed said, and not a single day of awe there. The Spanish swans lifting from the river: no ripples. To sit in a spring whose waters offer no prophecy.

The not-expected. The no-one-reading-your-mind. The-no-stopping-the-light-inside-the-beast-from-crumbling.

Long ago a fog came to settle on a meadow. And an old horse raised his head up to it . . . as it wafted down. Then that happy whinny at the moment he disappears.

"It Costs Nothing to Ride!"

This is how they get you on.
Given a seat, sit.
Be our guest, says the machine.
Be the bell a stranger rings.

Buckle up, babycakes! Twelve
is your age for 5 minutes
into which must fit the next 50 years.

The seat moves. **TomorrowWorld** keeps
to either side. Today passes through.

Isn't there a *Floored* in your future?

FUTURAMA (AT THE 1964 NEW YORK WORLD'S FAIR)

Our shrieks in its tunnel hang behind us. *Sit down and shut up,* shouts the conductor. Whoopee, here we go. Hurray, here we come. Its flashing lights boisterous, the lit-up hole beckons. Surely we'll all disembark at the other end. Surely I won't be the only one who doesn't fly off, fall off, or slip loose.

The littlest girl's squeals carry farthest and longest: "We're going to die! Don't let me die!"

It's just a ride, honey. Close your eyes, says the man from the future.

WE ROLL OUR EYES

Watching *A Wonderful Life* with our mother, we've made it to our thirties. We don't cry. When Mom dabs her eyes, we glance at each other and roll ours. My father dead, your father dead, and there'll be a third father you won't even meet. Because you'll be dead.

Mom's crying what she calls happy tears since of course there's an angel.

We sit tall, smirking beneath the oil portraits of our smiling teenage faces. *No one jumps; that's a stupid way to go* . . . is maybe crossing your mind. *Angel bullshit* crosses mine. We stare past the green plastic tree into the blizzard that appears benign but will turn out not to be.

Trees will fall, roofs collapse. We shake our heads. We're sure we're ready for it—fire and ice and carnage. All ready. So for it.

FINIS

There was a boy my sister loved. Gary. Well, we all loved Gary. They were 19. They got engaged. She tried on our mother's wedding dress: a size 12, a gown for a voluptuous woman of 1949, which our mother had been. "That gown just swims on you," my mother said. We agreed it needed to be taken in. My sister and I pulled out the bodice fabric, laughing. There was room in there for a whole extra set of breasts.

Then one day my sister came home with her own damn gown. Long tight-fitting sleeves with tiny grey pearl buttons to the elbow. A perfect size four. These days if I walk down the hall and make the mistake of glancing at the picture of her in it, I have to think of some chore to do in the cellar. Must clean shelves! Must glove up. Do *not* think of the dress.

Sweet funny Gary was what my stepdad called "a country boy." He'd eat a huge meal at our table then go lie on the living room floor, patting his belly in order, he explained, to make room for seconds.

He turned 20. My sister, just beginning to swirl inside the doctors' maze of medicinal options, quickly took matters into her own hands: upping her dose of this or that, then this *and* that. ER visits. Off and on a hospital stay to get her white count stabilized. Gary, at her bedside and knowing her fingers hurt, tenderly stroked her wrist. His parents grew alarmed. Was this the future that lay ahead for their son? They talked to our parents. How could their son "possibly take care of her"?

Then came the day my sister took back the dress. Gary had told her she should. That was all she'd say about it, her stern look insisting, Don't ask. *Maybe you should take back the dress.* "That's all he said," my sister told me. "Finis."

"LIVE WITH IT"

"Make me," my sister said.

"We have things that'll help you."

"I'll take everything you have."

"For your RA, we've got gold shots this week (but stay out of the sun) and next month synthetic pregnancy hormones, and of course we have Demerol, Percodan, Percocet, and you could go for it and try real pregnancy hormones (ha! ha!), and oh yes, we should try Imuran and Rheumatrex. For the Lupus, we'll obviously start with steroids and sometimes the antimalarials help (but again, stay inside!), and let's have a go at the ACTH injections, but remember we have lots of Oxy to get you by."

"I took all I could," she said.

"You can take some more."

"Make me," she said.

VAULT VS. FAULT

Four tries and four failures, and my classmates have gone from silent pity to loud guffaws.

Fifth attempt: I hit the springboard, leap, and drop back down. Down. Right in front of him. The bastard horse.

"You're over-thinking it," the teacher shouts. "Just *do* it."

Later, after school, I enter the dark gym and approach the horse. *You, sir, are a monster.* I kick him. I curse him.

But he only curses back. Strange grunts emanate from the leather-clad torso with a bomb ticking inside. I kick harder.

My stare apparently enters Deep Time. I have pushed too hard before. And too fast. Tick, tick, tick. Think not, I think.

My foot, my sprint, my spring—and I'm aimed into the ticking. It enters a mind's frazzled overdrive. I've pushed before, and quite badly. I'm the horror the horse sees. I'm everything he towers above.

WHAT STATE ARE WE IN?

"April," my mother tells the doctor.

Here're the pills then since she's failed the test. Down they fall into a well with slick wet walls. Coins climb up: two coppers . . . with the eyes they intend to cover quite in sight.

Our May state hovers, far off. Surely a seed for it grows deep in the future's dirt.

"Isn't this a night we set back the clock?" she wants to know. "Can't we sleep a little longer before our bare feet have to step over the hot red coals?"

MY SISTER'S SPIEL AS SHE GIVES HER LITTLE FRIENDS A TOUR OF OUR HOUSE

"This next room has the sewing machine I mentioned that can make a fancy dress if someone could just get that pedal to go up and down, and no, that other thing isn't a toad or a rock; that's my sister and that's her chair and yeah, her eyeballs are always stuck like that in a book, and don't look at her; this is a Do Not Disturb area. Try to pretend she's a ghost; that's what I do. But she bites sometimes. She used to kick. We've lived in twelve other states before this one. And right this way we have some weird stairs that pull down—voilà!—from a secret attic where some actual live animals live. We hear them at night—squirrels maybe—and they've eaten away half the face of our fake baby Jesus."

TRADING VEHICLES

I got a new Subaru and gave my mother my old Camry and she in turn gave her grandson her ancient Mazda. So all worked out. All was good. All was spring and everyone was tooling the drag in a refreshed forward thrusting. Perfected forwarding! All went well. As if a flawless plan had finally been put in effect.

All fine! *For twelve minutes*! A perfect twelve minutes. The perfect span of time to make a person believe in perfect, in plans, in a smooth ride down quiet roads.

720 seconds, then *whammo*. My nephew's new old Mazda hurtles through a red light—hard and bright, and the crazy crunch of cars.

We have to see the two totaled cars on the local news—at 4, 6, and 11. We have to hear three times "a miracle that everyone walked away."

My mother's *mea culpa* begins immediately and goes on for weeks. She's sure it's her fault, sure something had gone bad in the engine, a loose screw, sure she'd heard a pinging, a funny hum . . . .

I wake up to more trades up and down—dishes and cars and money changing hands—and someone snarling about "a screw loose." And *Please*, I'm telling myself as the dream ends, *just pay attention. Those lights! Those lights!*

MISTER ED SAYS, "STOP GABBING & GET ME SOME OATS"

Mister Ed wants Wilbur to understand that fibs are fine if they contribute to the greater marital good. He's talking *harmony*! Harmony is what we need. But lies are okay, of course, if they're on behalf of the horse. The famous mister.

At first my sister and I admire Ed. His plain-spokenness. His multilingual dexterity. (He speaks Spanish *and* he can translate "cat.")

But eventually we come to despise Ed: a braggart full of disdain for women, a joyful sneakiness, and a horrid singing voice. Still, she would like to ride him; I would like to feed him.

With a beautiful simplicity and, always in the last two minutes, Ed solves adult kerfuffles. And how *now*? My sister and I inch closer to the screen.

Wow! His voice booms out. It'll wake us on far-flung future side streets. He's awful and he's brilliant.

"You *kids*," Ed scoffs, "it's too early to hit the hay and too late to eat it."

Entertainment for Everyone!

re then!
rdines in a tin
—headless
ies in an oily row.
them or go
gry, says
father.

Repent! Repent!—
waved in our faces
on sloppy signs.
Repent *what*?
Poisonings? De-
flowerings by
a swan?

Famished was
the family. Here
comes the fishy
sustenance. Close
your eyes. The sea
swallows back,
swallows down.

The flushed-out
meadows burned:
still votive on the
breeze. We were
on our way—after
a bite—to visit
the oracle.

Couched in an Era

DRESSING

The grief had made my hair—just around the forehead—break off at the scalp. Dressing for my sister's funeral, I pulled long strands from my comb as if it belonged to someone irradiated. I jabbed pearls in my ears, two posts in two holes, suddenly remembering the long night of half-sleep with the windows open and the sounds wafting in: the great horned owl's squawk as she went for the last of the barn kittens, the one she'd saved all summer, and its final mewls growing strangely acquiescent, almost calm—a purr, a hum.

HOW HIGH *ARE* YOU?

"Oh high enough to hear a soft saxophone. But it's coming through bird voices!"

Please tell me. Super high? I can't handle another ER all-nighter.

"Not high enough to fall, or fall *hard* anyway. Not high enough for you to worry. Don't worry."

Yeah, I'd prefer that actually. A life. One of no worries, one away from this pile of horseshit.

"Thanks for caring."

Those hospital lights are so bright. Don't you hate them? All that glare.

"You should have a short puff yourself of something and chill the hell out."

I get so sad in there at 3 a.m. Down, you know, so far—

"Sis,   these birds.   They're   truly   fantastic!"

—down, like deep underwater. 3 a.m. is always bad.

"3 a.m. is always way too high."

ANOTHER STUPID SKY STORY

My sister explains to someone that she has lupus, and the someone says that means *wolf*, an animal my sister says she hates, and I toss in that Lupus is also a constellation. I point into the dark. A wolf's impaled on a pole held by a centaur. But we're too far north to see.

Why? someone wants to know. *A meal for later? A sacrifice?* Since the stars of Lupus have no names, they're no help.

Across the South American dark the wolf drips from the stick. He'd sacrificed a child and sampled her small entrails. His punishment: to drip drip drip.

Criminy. Why's the poor old sky have to be full of such gore?

Duh. *Why* is why we stand around staring into it.

HE WORE A BADGE

The Quaker friends sat in a circle that had a chair for me and no questions, and the circle said, Let's just be quiet here for forty minutes and see how that feels, see if some of what circles might enter and make our circle spin.

I'd cried my way there. My sister was dead. I was suddenly in charge of the Post-Death Proceedings. With no info, with nary a tip. I came for the circle and sat in it. Nothing entered. I cried my way home.

Her boy was ten, and what was there to do but lie to him about how the end had come to her? For her. Me saying she's "with the Lord now" and seeing his response rise as if in all caps across the clear slate of his face: *You. Are. An. Idiot.*

Post-Death, I was in charge of nothing. I drove him to the airport and as a bolt of thunder started a rain, an attendant put a badge on the boy and sent him up the metal stairs and into the sky and to a far-off father he barely knew.

IDIOT

The more I try not to be one, the more I am. And the more I am, the more I'm happily here for an hour in a new hairdo and Jackie's special mascara so my eyes feel big enough to pull in the entire Cutthroat Trout my husband has brought home and unwrapped in the bloodbath sundown.

The bright scales of one. The soft kiss of the other. A hand in my new hair, and no need to watch the knife slit open the belly. My glitzy lashes flutter. No need to be who I'd been an hour ago in *their*-story-become-*my*-story, and its sorrow and ire leeching, dripping. No need. No need to scrape the guts. This next hour melts the butter; this sizzle can't stop kissing the fish.

IN CHARGE OF NOTHING

From hour to hour I'd longed for more of Me-In-Charge, then for less, then Please, none. This lasted weeks. I'd stand in a purply dark—that swirling admixture of all colors—until the stars of lights in other houses flickered on.

Swirling too: the soft mutterings of child selves—mine, hers, his— and whose was whose? The all-voices circled as one indecipherable whisper.

Can a person suddenly know nothing? And be glad *of* it? Happily have *no* answers? And knowing zero, staring into it, can one pass through the hole of it as the stars in other houses flick off?

So late becomes too late. The child selves are confused. Whose father, which father, used to call out: *No! Steer into it! Steer* into *the skid.*

"FIRST WE MUST PUT ON OUR BROWS,"

my mother says. But she waves away the pencil I hand her. She likes a black ballpoint or the mascara.

Mascara's for lashes, I tell her.

"Lashes, brow slashes—who cares?"

I like this taupe color, I say, offering the pencil again.

She peers at its point. "That's grey, honey."

I'm her 65-year-old daughter but barely sixteen in her mind until she turns from the mirror and sees me. "You're my sister, *right?*"

I pause, assessing her face for a good answer. Giving up, I try the pencil myself easing my brow into a little arc of Say-*what?*

Forgetting her question, an old woman tugs twice at my sleeve. "Hey, could I use that thing when you're done?"

THE ENDLESS RETURN
OF LITTLE POMP

Sacajawea's dancing baby boy, Little Pomp, grew up to be a companion to a duke and the star of my sister's ninth grade book report. For tenth grade Little Pomp's revamped. He's spun around and lost his bearings. He pans for gold. A spell of pneumonia, and *ta-ta, so-long,* he's buried near the trail in Oregon where he died.

I fix her verbs. I mend punctuation. No teachers ever suspect since every year we're in another state. And so's Little Pomp.

He's baaaack! He's fathered babies on two continents. He's a momma's boy on a stamp we flip over and lick and love and send forth on a far western trek. The days stagger into years, seamlessly strewn across the wheated fields. Like us, Little Pomp was a kid had on the way, by the way.

MISTER ED HARPING
ON AGAIN ABOUT JONAH

Ed wants us to imagine Jonah, just imagine him sitting atop his host's heart, feeling its pulse beneath his buttocks, that whole whale of splayed-out suburbs leaning precariously in on what beats.

Among the entrails, minnows dip and dart like wrens—soundlessly daring as they dive into slow dissolve.

> Back home, stopped in a shade between two olive trees, Jonah had received the order. Maybe anyone standing so still feels that absorbed . . . as in a long final kiss.
>
> Though Ed insists the words weren't beautiful. Never were. You have to stand up and spit sand to repeat them. Stare into the hammering heart. Bang, bang, the red debt.

CODICIL OF SELECTED EXCISIONS: CHAPTERS I-IV

—the later Polaroid of no her in her room, but the space-of-her, which throbs as if sensing it's about to be ripped to shreds.

—I still have the red fox from Landerlunden. In fact, I've worn him— as the stole his hide became—for Halloween parties, happily demon- strating his mouth that opens and clips down, holding fast to his tail.

—the putting-on of brave faces. They pucker. They stick. They itch. They each have a little drawer that slides shut with a sweet click.

—I was overly warm and thinking of shucking my long yellow coat. Then, from afar a horse began whinnying his way into my waking.

—he wouldn't up the dose. "Maybe it's supposed to hurt," the doctor said. A refrain. Her rolled eye. My raised eyebrow. Someday I'm going to want to think further about this—not yet, though.

—I was a small person who believed she was bigger but not big enough for The Life. It seemed enormous and elaborate, a silk kimono for a giantess. Embroidered herons and dragons! I pull down a ladder from the ceiling, climb up, and see the garment still hanging in the attic. Scraps and insect-eaten rags drip from the hanger.

—I clean up after the afterlife. Doing an awful job. Still in charge of nothing. Across my wood floor, her flip-flop tracks continue beyond me. Before me. Behind me.

—A little light left. *I'll have that,* I say. Thus endeth the year of saying maybe, maybe.

Piss Pot of Gold Where Your Hideous Rainbow Ends

AT THE WORLD'S FAIR!

CINERAMA V.

TAKES YOU...

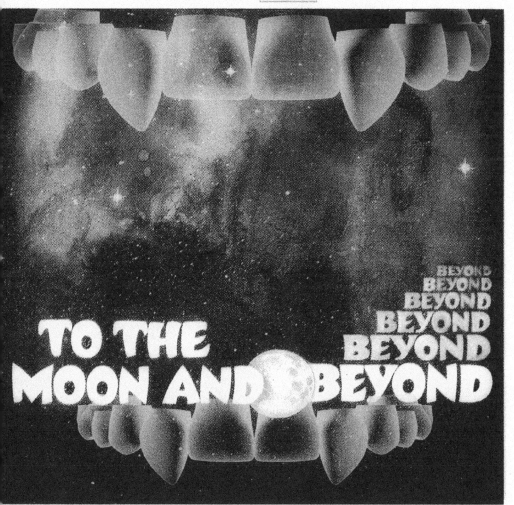

YOU will be propelled on the most fantastic, incredible voyage through billions of miles of space... from its utmost outer reaches... back to the Earth itself, and into the center of the minutest atom. Your sharpest teeth can't gnaw you out.

3 SHOWINGS EVERY HOUR
LOVELESS JOURNEYS AMONG WINDS OF ASH

AMONG THE DERVISHES (AT THE 1964 N.Y. WORLD'S FAIR)

Right beside my sister and me on International Avenue, the dervish dancers had whirled themselves into the non-material plane. Leaning, looking, we'd tried to feel ourselves where they were. Where *were* they?

"What world's fair?" my sister asked many years later. In a hospital dream, she was slowly coming down after hours up. I watched the doctor check her knee, which had been draining all day and was finally almost normal size.

My sister frowned at her knee as the doctor squeezed it. He wouldn't look at me.

I was supposed to *do* something. About *her*.

Make her.   Quit it.   Supposed to.   Make her.   Quit it!

He has no context, I thought. Everyone was without data and guessing. Even me. Even the preacher kid, he of the awful crew-cut who slipped almost stealthily into the room and knelt by her bed.

Cripes. I'd been asking her about the fair. Did she remember?

"Fair?" she repeated. Half here, half gone, she blinked from me to her knee on the damp pillow, as her doctor glowered and the kid checked his watch, bounced up, and swirled into the hallway's radiance.

MAYBE THE ATTIC'S NOT SO FAR AWAY AFTER ALL

"Your sister—she's such a character," friends would say. "A real live wire." Her cowgirl boots with feathers and turquoise beads up the sides. Her rowdy laughter spilling from upstairs, where, unbeknownst to me, she's just taken every painkiller I've ever stashed away, leftovers from years-ago dental procedures.

She's become a you who's become a—god help me—character of a character. I can't get any one *you* of her right. I cross through each *her* as soon as it's made. God, how vicious those black XXX's! She crawls around overhead, cursing me from the long gone attic in which mom's crèche has just become the dregs of a fabulous squirrel feast. *You pick it up! Fuck you, you pick it up.*

MY HUSBAND'S STORY FROM THE WAR

He only tells it when he's tipsy. A missile was in mind for a minute:
the captain's brief thought bubble that became an order.

Happy New Year, my husband was instructed to print on the side of
a bomb. His job for that particular 1969 December's end in Phước
Vĩnh. As company clerk, he was typist, painter, and ornate calligrapher
of placards for colonels' seats at steak dinners in Quonset huts.

And the soaring hardy har-har of the missiled message. The long
screech of *Haaap—eeee* passing over rice paddies in that sweltering
summer as already the *Haaap—eeee* raced towards a 45th year later in
a man's future, where the *New* and the *Year* never quite arrive—just
the punchline's boom, and then the boom's echo.

"WHAT'S YOUR PAIN SCALE?"

"Christ, not this again," my sister answers. "My scale's got gold lettering and two china goddesses playing teeter-totter. Each gal's sitting on a separate but identical shiny chrome plate."

My sister crosses her arms. "Shiny chrome!" A hurled gut blow. "Super shiny."

Loud sighs from the one we call "the nurse girl," who tosses her thick dark ponytail and slowly waddles off.

ON TWO GREEN NOODLES

"It's gotta be boring." My sister was staring up into a sheer blue sky. "Para-fucking-dise."

I shook my head. *I doubt either of us needs to fret about it.*

"All those goodie-goodies. . . ."

Lying atop a pair of green swim noodles, I was floating in the deep end. In my long days through short decades, there'd been this one time of plenty: quiet country acreage, a pool, a barn, a neatly tilled garden. No fire, no sizzle, no burn.

"Paradise—everything so evened out," my sister said. She'd been sitting on the pool steps, her head tipped back.

Hey, shouldn't you be in the shade? Isn't the sun like poison to you?

"I miss the sun." She slid into the water, keeping her face skyward, her ears under water.

I watched her wiggle lower. Into the good water. Blue above and below. The kind blue.

It was all almost over.

I, for one, had not a clue.

MOM AND THE AL-ANONS

They tell her to give dad an ultimatum. His booze or his wife—he had to choose. She did what they'd said. And, just as I'd guessed, that pissed him off. Not so much the choosing. Nor the giving up one or the other. But the ultimatum itself.

"Those Al-Anons," he said, "they've got her hoodwinked." Then he put his hands over his face. He said he still loved her. His tears embarrassed him. He said she couldn't handle my sister and my sister's baby by herself, and he could help. Said I should talk to her.

She never listens to me, I snapped. I wanted to get up and glide breezily out of the diner.

Stooped over his grilled cheese, he didn't seem so much sad, I thought, as pathetic. I thought that, then immediately despised myself for thinking it. As I do now, writing it. *Pathetic.*

Just weeks before in another restaurant, a swanky one, after loudly proclaiming his boss an asshole, he lost his last good job, an executive vice president. But there, in our diner, he shrugged. Said he'd already found another job. He was selling penknives, maps, and tiny flashlights to dime stores all over the Inland Empire. From across the table he passed me a vinyl packet of these items.

I gnawed my salad like a rabbit. *I'll talk to her,* I said between bites. He opened the packet and demonstrated how to operate the flashlight. *I'll talk to her, okay?* He showed me the blades of the small knife. *I said I would, alright? I will.*

MORE AND LESS

You may be thoroughly dead, but oh, here you freakin' *are*. Scoffing at the shoes in my closet. "Surely you wouldn't wear *these*?"

I study the blue denim loafers. Your voice drilling down: "Surely?"

All dead, you drift along so very half-dead, still scraping a chair across my hardwood floor, still smoking on a back step in the cold fog. Half-dead, you cough. You sigh. All gone, you mock my evening's culinary offering, "a most unsliceable lasagna."

DANG IT

I was a college student rushing to class. I'd overslept, had no coffee, and was dreading a pop quiz in Organic Fucking Chemistry. Ahead of me someone else was rushing too. A blind girl. She tapped a black cane in front of her, first on one side of a building's column, then on the other, and then bang!— she smacked right into it.

"Are you okay?" I hurried to her.

"Dang it," she said, still standing, rubbing her forehead. "What is this?" She touched the column, marveling at its porous texture and girth.

"Dang it," she repeated when I told her, then turned and walked carefully around it, and on.

I was in my third and last year as a pre-med student and finally accepting that I would never go to medical school. Apparently poetry needed all of me. I worked 3-11 in a hospital, got up early, and went to classes. I loved my life. And felt guilty about that. Why should *I* be happy? My sister had been put on a plane and flown to Dallas for a "miracle" rheumatoid arthritis cure our father had seen advertised in *The National Enquirer*. The cure involved massive doses of hormones and steroids. Returning home three weeks later, she was fifty pounds heavier. The miracle doctor had been "dismissed" from the hospital staff while she lay there bloated, sore, and wondering why *her*.

I loved my life. I was away from *them*. But in random moments—in the shower, taking a pee, eating a yogurt—I worried about them. My life. It seemed to have a grown a shape, a thing I didn't hold but one that held me, moving me in and out of the enormous, bustling world.

Over the years the image of that blind girl's collision often returns. I see the cane tap so perfectly to the sides of the column and I feel my later self trying to wake up my early self, to make her shout, "Hey, look out!" But the words still stick. I'd been walking through the world but I wasn't in it. The girl goes forward. The girl smashes into the thing right in front of her.

MY REPORT CARD: "PATIENCE—BELOW AVERAGE, NEEDS IMPROVEMENT"

Almost sixty years later my third-grade teacher still scolds me in dreams where I'm often in line for something, fidgety and foot-tapping and complaining about the *slow people; what is* wrong *with them?!*

"It's life," the teacher says. "It sucks"—her voice becomes more of a beep bouncing through the people-heavy line, which grows longer and slower by the second. "It's-life-it-sucks" circles on a beep-beep loop.

Then suddenly: "What're you working on now?" she asks.

Backstory, I say.

"Whose?"

Oh, you know, the story's be-hind, *hers, his, ours, mine. The uni-verse's.*

"You're still in love then?" she asks, or was it, "You're still in life then?"

I shrug. I feel like a dog on a chain, and suddenly, a far-off end-of-the-line someone yanks the chain, and I slide a titch forward.

MISTER ED PRONOUNCES HUMANS PAINFULLY SLOW

"You humans, it only takes you twenty-plus *years* to reach the really deep hole, then a bunch more years to get up the nerve to touch it, let alone rub it, or just kiss it and leave it be."

Wilbur is bewildered, staring, unfazed by Ed-talk, out the window. Wilbur seems not to know that Ed of course has made Wilbur *his* horse.

Ed says, "I've got to go bet on a filly, but first, one more thing about the darkest wound. A lot will be clear about it right away—by how it brightens or darkens as you get closer, or maybe it gives off a series of winces."

Here Ed demonstrates the winces, degrees *of:* the Regular Wince—ears flapping; Large Wince—haunches shuddering, eyes blinking.

"The rain is so lovely," Wilbur says with a loud sigh.

Ed's already on the phone with his bookie.

Thus endeth today's episode as ye ol' Cheery Song clomps in.

You'll love *Walt Disney's* magic touch at
AUTOPSY REPORT IN PROGRESSLAND

VI.

Delightful Carousel of Progress—*What?*
You can't wake up? Can't get
your old lady shoes to walk you
onto the New Day's shore?

Mammoth Sky-Dome Spectacular
Your heart's quite cold when it's
taken out and weighed. Colder
still when it goes back in.

Awe-inspiring Atomic Fusion
If you swallow every pill in the
hilarious house, you'll arrive
under it, laughing your head off.

Fascinating Medallion City.
**Everything here was for sale:
YOUR MONEY OR YOUR LIFE.**

Then

I DUCKED OUT THE BACK DOOR

Fight or flight. Something we probably learned early. Although flight usually proved easier, fight might be what we'd try first. "No, we're not moving to Connecticut." Our hands on our hips. "We're going to live with Nani."

"Nani!" Our parents collapsing with laughter in the kitchen.

Once, distraught about leaving my little friends, I ran away. I made myself pick one doll (Tiny Tears) and put her in a squat brown suitcase. I passed my four-year-old sister napping in her room, slipped outside, and traipsed through the neighbors' backyards until I came to a busy street. I knew where the busses stopped. I had twelve dollars. I was sure Nani would welcome me back to our real home in Virginia, our real home before this new father had moved us to New York, where my southern drawl was the subject of much fourth-grade ridicule.

"I can't believe you'd leave your little sister," my mother shouted as she pushed me inside the car. (No doubt a neighbor had seen me and ratted me out.) "Just look how you've made her cry. She's hysterical."

But she wasn't. Staring at me, she went silent, as if I'd just returned from the dead.

Eight years later when she tried it herself, I scoffed. "They think they're God," I snapped. "And you can't fight God."

"Yes, you can," she snapped back. Then she schlepped her knapsack to her friend Patty's house, where, secretly the parents had agreed, she could stay for a few days.

I don't recall how they pulled her back. But of course they did. Of course we pressed on. Dragging Dad's boat behind us. Down the Crazy Woman Mountains, over the Rockies, and through the Selkirks.

For a while my sister fought her way through adulthood. She'd put on her nurse's uniform. . .long hours, long days. Then for a few years she quit fighting and only wanted to fly. Finally she stumbled upon a way to do both at the same time.

MID-DAY, MID-WAY
ON THE CONTINUUM

My sister had been dead for seven years, and my mother was telling the boy how his mom had always preferred her eggs gooey, and he turned and smiled, not remembering this. He asked if she'd ever heaped on hot sauce the way he does.

I went back to watching rain out a window, feeling my eyes well up even as the other two laughed a little, recalling how my sister could go throw up from one too many of the blue pills, then come back to the table and finish a meal.

Ha, ha. He asks me something. We were seven years away right then from his own bowing out. And was the germ of it already secretly in his mind?

What?

"Aunt Nance, want cheese on yours?"

And when I nod, he flips both fried eggs at once and pronounces "perfectamente" upon the landing, the lunch, and the whole day since finally, he tells us, finally he'll be wrapping burgers for another fifteen cents an hour.

BROKEN RIBS

Two on the left, one on the right. Goners. For good. From here on. I show a friend: *Here, with your fingertips, press right here on the side.* Her eyes widen as she feels the jagged place where the bones went crunch in the middle of the night. *Even before the pain,* I tell her, *the loud crunch jerked me awake.*

Beyond Repair.

Drink more milk and lift some weights. Live with it. It will teach you how. You don't need to do a thing. No, there'll never again be a comfortable way to lean back on a chair. Don't stew on it.

Yeah, that's the way, that's right, that's how.
Share the space.
The live-with-it kicking in.
The *that* in the *that's nothing.*

A tiny nothing. A tiny nothing that slipped loose from the infinite one into which my sister and her boy walked, their arms out, feeling nothing, the boy zombie-like behind his mother.

Roll over. Cry out. Go back to sleep.
U   R   A   Live   with   It
  U   Alive
      It.

TINY TEARS

On the day my sister was born, my mother and stepdad presented me with a Tiny Tears doll. Here, they said, you should have a baby too.

Not quite five, I stared at the secret hole (in the throat!) where the water went. Oh. So there'd be tears. Oh, so *crying* was *okay*.

No matter how much everyone tried to stop the crying, clearly they also *wanted* the crying. Not to cry was *not* normal.

I squirted the eyedropper's water into the hole, watching the eyes blink twice and discharge two fat tears that took their sweet time drifting down cold unflinching cheeks.

You bathe and dress and feed a baby, and still it cries.

My infant sister cried.

My baby did too.

No matter how much we rocked and sang, or tickled, patted, and cooed, all the babies cried. *Hush, baby.* Ever shriller sobs. *Come on, baby.* Wet sobs. *Buck up, baby.* Breathless sobs.

So many babies. Babies by the millions—they wake up and blink up and cry some more.

YES YOU ARE

In the dream I'm supposed to save someone. A house is on fire. I'm supposed to hurry. I need to get her out of there. My sister. Or so I've been instructed.

But my sister's standing right in front of me. In my kitchen. A tiny kitchen from decades ago.

"You're dead," I say.

So what? She opens a cupboard door.

What's she looking for? Drugs, I think. Then I hear that fire crackling in the distance. I need to hurry.

She opens another door.

I catch her eye. In it I see the calm void of the past tense—biding its time, waiting at the end of the now.

BACK TO VIRGINIA

Virginia: the same destination my mother had when she herself ran away. Living there in Columbus, Wisconsin (move #13 for our family), my mother proclaimed one night she was "fed up with all the drinking in this house." She packed a suitcase. She'd just discovered my stepdad had spiked the punch for a high school pre-homecoming party in our living room. And though 18 (my age then) *was* the legal drinking age at that time in Wisconsin, my mother was aghast. Seeing my teenage friends stumbling and fumbling, my mother turned and stomped upstairs. Meanwhile Dad was urging a young woman to dance atop the coffee table (which she did!).

I could hear my mother upstairs slamming doors. Then the backdoor banged shut. My friends were sneaking sips of punch—pink lemonade and vodka—to my 14-year-old sister.

"Mom's gone," my sister came into the kitchen to tell me.

I looked out the window. *She'll come back,* I said. *The car's still here.*

Then my sister mentioned the suitcase.

I didn't even say goodbye; I just got in the car. I had an idea where my mother would be. I drove six blocks. And there she was. In the Chevron station. Waiting for the bus. It'd take her to Madison, and from there, she told me when I sat down next to her, she was going back to Virginia.

If that's what you want, I said.

"Everyone in that house is snookered," she said.

I'm not, I lied.

This wasn't the first time she'd packed up and tried to leave, and there'd be another couple times before the leaving stuck.

Cars streamed in and out; bells buzzed; phones rang. Silently we sat there watching, waiting for a bus that, as it turned out, wasn't due for three hours.

"Your friends will be too drunk to dance." My mother touched my homecoming dress, a dress I can't recall in the least. We shared a candy bar and a coke, something we still do. We sat inside the clanging world.

She was tired, she finally said, and I replied something like, *Don't you want to stretch out in your own bed,* and she said something like yes.

IN A CORNER OF OUR GARAGE

My husband saves the handles of his father's tools—the axe, the hoe, the shovel. Just the wood: sanded, polished, gleaming, and standing apart from, and indifferent to, their missing metal ends.

Seeing them reminds me of the sweet old man and the one time I saw him tear up. He'd just fished out of his garbage bin my husband's box of Army medals, the box my husband had brought up from his parents' basement and casually tossed in the trash.

The single tear down the old man's face in the moonlight . . . as my husband motions from a window, *No, let them go.*

And so they went.

Years earlier I'd asked him about them, a conversation that went something like this:

> *Where are they?*
> He shrugged.
> *What were they?*
> He rolled his eyes.
> *When did you last see them?*
> In a headache last week, in a bad dream last month.

WHAT WAS LEFT IN THE CRÈCHE

Thick cobwebs in the manger, and beneath them the black-bellied spiders—broken, dead where they'd dropped. Bits of sheep wool that had been the hair of St. Joe. His crooked crook in pieces. Pigeon scat: dust of. Two tiny glass eyes: one brown, one blue. Shriveled plastic parts—of ultra-tame animals and miniature holy people. Ear, snout, thumb. Foot, face, tail. The feel of the elements pressing in. Thoroughness: taking its time. Thoroughness was how we liked it and how it all worked out in the end.

MISTER ED'S GREATEST WISH: AERONAUTICAL CONTROL

Wilbur tries to get Ed to fetch, but Ed's having none of it. Ed wants to fly a plane! That Ed. Such a goofball. When, outside the psychiatrist's window, Ed parades by in hilarious disguise—movie star sunglasses and beret!—Wilbur cracks up, which causes him to fail the psychiatric exam and so can *not* receive his pilot's license, a pilot who'd of course have allowed Mister Ed to take the controls and soar.

Sheesh. Cross-legged on the floor, two girls nod and snicker.

That Ed. He never takes no for an answer. Ed *shall* fly!

He steals a plane and lifts into the off-white clouds of a TV sky. *No.* The response a clever mind schemes to dismiss. Check. ✓ The sisters glance at each other. Got *it*. ✓ ✓

One sister fears for Ed's safety and that of the townsfolk below, while the other sister whinnies a horsey laugh the fearful one will hear trilling loudly through dreams even decades after the laughing one's dead.

Then suddenly from the stolen plane, Ed leaps out and parachutes down, descending through billowing whites and soft greys as the ever-aftering melody tries to drown out the sky's silence.

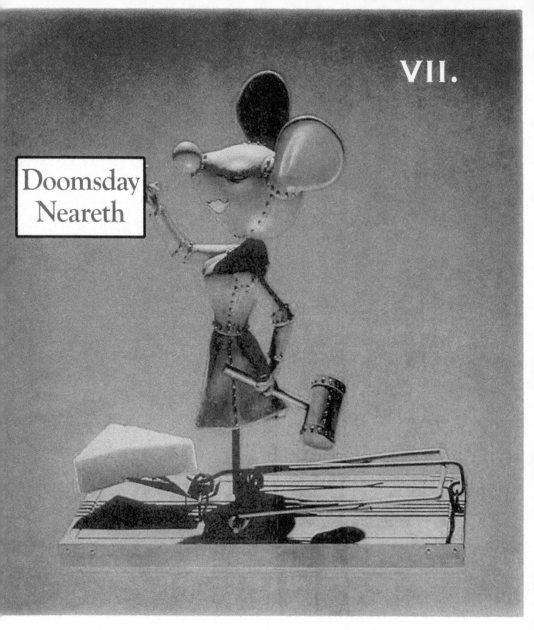

VII

Doomsday
Neareth

Beware A Picketer

lthough the others' signs may exclaim the apocalypse in purples,
erhaps "Oh" is all yours has to say. "Not Yet," reads your sister's.
he died years ago, but she holds her placard in front of her girl-face,
hen shakes it in front of yours. She was from the end-times, and Oh,
he was back with a vengeance.

THE END THAT KEEPS COMING (AT THE 1964 NEW YORK WORLD'S FAIR)

The People for the Apocalypse walk their signs—*The End Cometh!*—up Avenue of Commerce and down Truman Promenade.

What will make them stop? New shoes? Old Money?

My sister's six. She's tired and wants to rest.

I reread the words, making no sense. What *End*? What *Cometh*?

But I can tell it's tough work the sign-carriers do, trudging back and forth, trying to unmake what's already hard-wired and sizzling in the sun.

Their signs point all ways at once, then briefly disappear as they're marched behind The Astral Fountain.

ON A DAY BETWEEN

On a day that fell between my sister's suicide and her funeral, I did a thoughtless, terrible thing. Through a window open behind me, the breezes had grown cooler, and I leaned back to wind the window shut. A handle I had to turn, gradually bringing the glass closer to the screen. Cranking. Not watching. Cranking harder. Just my hand behind my back, turning.

A little give, and then none. Something was stuck between the glass and screen. When I stood up to investigate, a sick feeling set in.

One of *them*. Those two mourning doves whose loud cooing so often woke my husband and me. At sunset they visited our back patio. I'd smashed one of them. My hand pressing. Hard. Too hard. Fingers around that slim handle. Not thinking. Doing.

I rushed outside. I heard myself screaming, my face twisting so strangely it hurt. My husband came running. I pried the window back and the dove fell at our feet. We stared down at it. One wide black eye blinked up at us. *Her!* the blink shouted. *Her, her, her.*

If you think the bird rose again and fluttered off, you'd be wrong.

REGULAR LIFE

My sister had been dead for three months and my husband and I wanted a short time away from "grief central." We paid a grad student to stay in our house and look after our four cats and nine angora rabbits.

Well, of course, in our absence, a rabbit died. "Bury her out back beyond the garden," I told the student on the phone. "Bury her deep so the coyotes don't eat her."

The student crying. Me trying to tamp down both my tears and my temper, which felt familiar now. Regular life.

That little grey rabbit. The doe who'd once peed on then stomped one of her babies through the cage's wire mesh flooring. Something wrong with that kit? Not enough milk for four, only for three? Rabbit-world mysteries abound.

This evening I pick up her tiny skull from my bookshelf. Of course the student hadn't buried her deep enough. Rubbing my thumb across the brittle bone, I think of the coyote, hungry out there in a 30-year-old, far-off dark. His long snout nods up. The decades clang together. Who holds the dried-up dregs of his meal? Who arrives now at the opposite end of anger?

SPOKANE FIRESTORM, 1991

I. Try to Think a Happy Thought

Please, I tell myself. *Just try. Think* one *happy thought.* Somehow my husband and I, and our home, have survived the firestorm. Six days of shifting winds, sirens, and us dragging shovels across smoky embers in the moonlight.

We survived. Somehow. Standing with garden hoses on our rooftop as ever grittier clouds circled. I even survived my fear of heights and another fear I hadn't known I had: flames.

Try to focus on the positive, I tell myself when it's over. Think a happy thought. You're *okay.* Your family's fine. Your hysterical mother and frantic sister drove through flames on either side of the county road to "help"—first by loading all your husband's suits into his truck cab, and then, as a sudden afterthought, by rounding up all four cats and putting them in atop the suits.

"Okay," they'd signaled to me on the roof. Shouting: "Okay, we're all ready to go. *Now.* All *ready.*"

Five minutes, I kept answering. *Just hold on!* I had the cold hose in my hot hands, spraying the ridiculous cedar shakes. Three houses down, my neighbors' house was ablaze. We watched it go—in two minutes.

Happy. I tried Happy. Tried to locate the grateful person I should have been? Where *was* Happy? Happy felt hard. Even the trying felt trying. Surely Happy couldn't live in all that smoke and ash, which, apparently, live forever.

II. I See Her Up There on the Roof

Fierce. The former me. Fierce to save. I catch the drift of her back-then thinking: *Oh well, I suppose it's about time. Gotta get going. Drive away from all of it. Everything. Time then. Almost. Time now.*

But another me just stands there. Conjoined to that hose. Holding it against her waist. Kooky umbilicus. Inside the hose was all the *real* fierceness, the kind that can drench terror.

JUST   TRY   NOT   TO   LOOK   DOWN.

Down below was everyone. Everything. Four cats, nine rabbits, one husband. One sister, one mother, one nephew. The swimming pool a generator was helping the hose to empty. Barn, garden, truck, car, house. Everything alive. Everything thriving.

I see the woman on the roof inhale a pine-pitchy smoke. She has *no* idea.

In a year, her sister will subtract herself from the Everything. Her nephew will start down a trail into lostness. The elderly mother will age ten years in ten months. But the gal with the hose trusts in the fierceness. She bends the fierceness, aims it towards where the fire seems headed. *Water, more water! Harder. Faster. Water will save everything.*

III. My Back-Then Thinking

It arose out of blind trust in bad winds that promised to shift. *Soon, soon,* sang the old thinking.

Soon-soon becomes a two-syllable word-bubble that drifts skyward into the evening's dark.

Then quickly the *soon-soon* flits off, soars out of earshot.

Surely the second *soon*, the one retaining a soft lightness from an olden-day ebullience, buoys them along towards a quiet blackness.

Of course this happens just before the other *soon* shoves them both into the brightly swirling emptiness.

IV. Suited

The mother and younger sister make speedy decisions because the older daughter, the loony one on the roof, is *so slow*. Because she "over-thinks everything." Said with sighs by the mother, with rolled eyes by the sister.

Never mind the photos; forget the computers, the jewelry, the family china. The man's suits must be saved from the fire. The man will need to go back to work ASAP. Suited, he will be fine. Suited, he will step into the office. He will shrug off catastrophe. Suited, he can march into bad winds, even the winds the worst fire makes all on its own.

Suited, he will see the next one coming.

But shirtless that day on our roof, he'd called down from his peak to mine, "Your mother and sister are nuts. They've just stuffed all my suits in the truck."

And both of us—shirtless now, 25 years later, and stepping from a cool lake into warm sunlight—laugh and shake our heads, remembering. A quarter century in embers behind us. Is what was coming finally here? A shrug, a smile, a little happy—what took these so long? To get here? To find us?

DOWN EQUALS IN

The mind-numbingly perky *Mister Ed* song hurls itself at me, and here comes 1961 offering handshakes and wearing those same white gloves I was forced to wear in that "Year of the Neat & Nifty," as the bug-nibbled magazine cover calls it.

"... answers that you'll endorse." *Oh please. Oh Ed, you jerk.*
You prick my optic nerve. You pinch the worn-out dregs of it.

Carol yanks off her gloves. Ed talks behind her back, and she his. But now she shouts at befuddled Wilbur, "There must be an explanation for this! There *must.*"

"She's a dope," my sister says, and I nod, and we twist the knob that should have *softened* the song, but which clearly only screwed it deeper in.

VIII.

3e Happy, the Everybody-Smiles said.
This is our winsome look. Wear it.
This, a determined smile. Don it.

Every 7.5 seconds a baby is born in the U.S.A.
Every 18 seconds someone dies in the U.S.A.
Every 11 seconds our population increases by 1.

Mister Giant Tabulator, are you still
ticking? Tally-man, if you count me in,
you must count my sister out. We are
The Cancellators. Who knew?

Are those seconds in earth time?
Here's how to curl upon oneself
like a leaf. Thus is a space
made ready for a dream
we know as sleep.

he **EQUITABLE** Life

IN THE AFFIRMATIVE

The mother winds thin cold fingers around the daughter's warm ones. "And I had two children? That's all?" The daughter travels up and out and watches herself nod. She's one of the two. The living, kicking one.

The mother says she wishes she'd had more. "A whole passel." The daughter says her sister's first name, and the mother supplies the last but with a small crisp question mark hovering at the name's end, where the blackness pours in and fingers on fingers tighten.

WHICH MOTHER, WHAT MOTHER?

I may not have mentioned it, but my first sister was Black. I was three and she was four. Her mother was my mother when my mother was at work. (My father's car, crossing tracks, was run over by a train. Instantly my mother was a widow. Since his death she'd been trying, and failing, to salvage his business. Restaurant supplies. Soaps he'd whip up in grandmother's cellar.)

My Black sister and I liked to play in the ravaged flowerbeds. Dolls made of stems and blossoms. One day my mother came home to find the other mother had bathed us both, then used rags to set ringlets into my damp blonde hair. And my real mother shook her head and laughed. "Rags!"

In another year she'd meet a new father and marry him and for a little while he'd be known in our family as the *step farther,* which I guess was the best I could utter it.

I still recall my mother's wild laughter in the kitchen, and neither my dark sister or I could guess what was funny. Nor, apparently, could my other mother whose black face went blank, causing my uncertainty to rise about which mother loved me most, or which I should love most: the pale one still laughing or the black one bending and whispering as she lifted each rag from my hair, "Beautiful, beautiful."

NINJA WARRIOR

I take my six-year-old nephew with me to visit a friend. She has a son his age, and immediately the boys are playing in a roomful of toys, a room nothing like the temporary basement space my nephew has in his grandmother's house while my sister's in the hospital. For our boy everything's always temporary. Everything can change, will change, out of nowhere, in one second.

As my friend and I sip tea, I mention that I like the victory yelps of the boys. Apparently a G.I. Joe has been assassinated by a turtle person. I can't discern which boy shouts and which one shoots.

Cookies are served outside, where the boys build a cardboard fort. My friend is still a poet, but tiring of the life. Soon she'll turn to painting and later to beadwork. Only the making makes her happy.

Driving away that day, my nephew and I wave out our windows. Then I see in the rearview my friend and her son running after my car.

"My ninja! My ninja!" her son shouts.

I stop and look at my nephew. But I don't even have to ask. The answer's sprawled across his face.

Was this the moment I began to turn from him, to sense the hopelessness, the futility of trying? The first time I felt my heart constrict? Felt he'd already become someone who cared nothing about consequence?

"Oh," he says, pulling the plastic warrior from his pants pocket. "Oh, I forgot I had this." He hands it to me.

Sorry is all I can manage when I pass it out the window. *Sorry* was a vapid word grating against gravel, a word I'd next have to instruct him to say, which he'd do with an enormous grin as the word snapped liked a white sheet in a brief wind.

THEY SAY

I tromp through leaves on my late fall walk and try to shuck off a cold and hellish fog.

Do your Ever-More byways get as same-old, same-old as mine?

I guess I'm talking about hell's hallways, the ones, someone tells me, you'll be pacing forever. Whatever forever *is*.

My making it to a vast old age, so what? These bright reds & golds— Too Very Here! Hard to shut up! Hard to hold still! I can't do what you did. Can't get any closer to the silence you keep so well.

Shut up and hold still—just what we'd scolded you to do. Back when. Back when you'd never obey as perfectly as you do now.

MAKING IT TO VAST OLD AGE, SO WHAT

I dress my cat in a baby bonnet, then feel the infusion of his disdain for all that is insipidly human and most alive in a frilly disguise.

Through the clear yellow eyes of underworld lamps, he looks inside me for who I will be when dead. Will he want to eat me?

I untie his ribbons and lie down on my belly so he can climb upon my butt and survey the enormity of his ridiculous kingdom.

WITH RIBBONS UNTIED,

I float on a battered quilt towards a brick wall, pat the wall (*nice wall!*), and float back . . . .

. . . wake, put a little rouge on a pale cheek, spit a kiss into love's ocean, and then lie back and bathe in the funnies . . . in the uproar.

What I said and she said are on hold so I can sigh for my friend who's "out of frickin' lip-gloss," so I can nod to the one with the raised arthritic middle finger, so I can smear a little red smudge on the other cheek, the one I've miraculously managed to turn.

"MIXED TOXICITIES"

Cause of my nephew's demise. I read it on the death certificate. *Mixed. Toxicities.*

Months later I find his backpack—left, forgotten, having been pushed far under mom's guestroom bed, where he'd laid down for an after-noon nap.

Called for dinner, he slept on.

When my hands slip inside the backpack pockets, I feel the pill bottles. My hands touch one bottle, two, three, and then in another pocket, a fourth bottle and a fifth.

My hands. Suddenly resolute and on their own, they refuse to lift a single bottle from a single pocket. Instead, the fingers count the bottles again. The name of this or that—to the hands it's moot. The bottles were all empty. To the hands, this was the point.

DESCENDANTS

My sister and I grew up believing we were descendants of William Penn. Because our mother said so. For my sister's short life and much of mine, we trusted we'd trickled down that way. Heirs to something quiet . . . petals dropped from a tree in a late great age of ice.

The earth tilts a tad and spins a titch faster. I'd believed a *story*. But a little digging into actual facts, and WTF, we weren't even English! Scots-Irish for me (with a dollop of Mongol thrown in!) and my (half) sister with a heaping helping of German, some old storekeeper, a man on the corner, the *winkel*.

Apparently I come from a line of people who like to make shit up. My mother could live so hard in the made space she'd forget the making. Her father's last name was Penn, so voilà—an assumption becomes a decrepit rubber-band-fact wound around other rubber-band-facts.

The band breaks. (They all do. No matter.) My mother shrugs when I mention the Great Khan. No, I am *her* daughter.

She knows the gravesite where she'll go. By my sister's, by her boy's. My mother's name is already chiseled in . . . with the start date and blank space for the other. She stands next to the stone and passes down the half-dead lilacs so I can arrange them by my sister's first name, which was one she rarely used.

The earth spins. A thousand miles an hour! Christ, no wonder these flowers shiver in the wind, in the rapid turning we're too inside of to even feel. Shivers atop shivers—Mom and I, amid the flags and the flowers, half-braced against the iced breezes in the half dark.

ED SAYS JONAH ONLY GOT SPIT OUT SO HE COULD SPEAK UP

There in the belly, the notion of continuing-to-be at odds with having-to-do. The cave heaves slowly in, slowly out.

Dawn to dusk, men and women work up a great black dirt. Air it out. Pat it down. Backs to it. Spades flailing.

Someone else's edicts: first to sit with them like corpses still uncrossed to the other side, then to deliver them from your own mouth.

Or to hoist up from one belly into another what's eating you.

> The immensity's eye takes an eternity to open. The salt foam laps at the lens.
> Ships, sails, shores—nothing registers. Lie back then and learn to love the cell.
> Or get up, flick off the viscid gore, and check the hour. As if some appointment to keep with a Pharisee. As if you were still alive among the living.

CODICIL OF SELECTED EXCISIONS: CHAPTERS V-VIII

—I pull a shade off a lamp. Staring at the shade. What to do with it? Wash it or wear it? Horse teeth smile in my window.

—flushing away that mother rabbit's half-frozen, Vienna-sausage-sized baby had seemed so easy. Except for the faint heartbeat. A few beats. In my palm. Except for that.

—I was a small person and The Life kept gathering heft as it moved ever closer, so close that one day I accidentally killed a dove and then the froth of The Life was all around me, on all sides, and finally I was in in in.

—the phone call a month before she died. She didn't want anything. Did not. Quit asking. Nothing's up. She was fine. Just saying hi. My incredulity was killing her. We hung up. Something seemed up.

—I was going in circles; my eyes felt irradiated. Looking and looking. No her in the blast radius but I felt sure she could clear a path, or at least locate the path to the path.

You're dead, I say.

I'm not. No matter how hard you think I am.

—when one speaks from afar, one always says *was, were, then*. One says *her* and means *you*, says *you* and means *her*, calls oneself *one*, ad nauseam.

—someone hated the coming story. She was my sister.

Time Capsule Components

BOTTLE EXHAUSTED OF AIR, FILLED WITH ARGON AND SEALED WITH FUSED CRYSTAL COVER

BOTTLE SEALED IN LEAD CONTAINER, WHICH IS ENCASED IN CARBORUNDUM CYLINDER

...FILLED WITH ASBESTOS

TIGHTLY WRAPPED SCROLL INSERTED IN MOUTH

IX.

SCROLLS UNROLL TO UNIFORM SIZE AGAINST MONEL METAL BANDS

NECK NARROWED FOR SEALING

CONTAINER MADE OF RODS OF FUSED QUARTZ CRYSTAL

RECORDS WRITTEN ON WHITE JAPANESE PAPER WITH CHINESE INK

BRAIDED ASBESTOS CUSHIONS BANDS

LEES? DEEP DOWN IN THE BOTTOM OF THIS HERE? TRUST ME. LOOK HARDER.

PLEASE, WON'T SOME OTHERS LIKE US (BUT NOT EXACTLY!) COME FIND US?

WHAT WE LOVED
IN THE LAST LIFE

The Mood Ring! It's coming to me. About to be invented and passed from my sister's finger to mine, circa 1973. My grey mood would soon dim her turquoise glow.

We wanted violet! We expected violet! Trusted violet. The ring could fit her, then me. All was adjustable. And surely a color never lies. A color makes promises. A color claims wisdom, nobility, magic and oh so much more.

Forty years later the ring's gone lime green, off on its own in a dusty box. As *she* is: her hands bare, her hands folded.

I come round in a mood of burnt umber: as if small mood embers burn on . . . though fewer each day. Fewer. Each day. Each of the still-waking days, each of the barely-woken.

UP TO SPEED: MOREOVER

Buba's keeping her night light on—that's new. *It's okay.* Lean with me over the face. Say it with me: *Everything's fine.* Her ninetieth birthday's leered and licked and passed.

As long as the clock ticks, the teeth in the glass won't chatter. The china bluebird won't chirp. Prayers for her two daughters' two souls trail off . . .

as the wall with our portraits on it crumbles. You first and me behind—and under such scrutiny of our vigilant avatars!— we make our ways out of her living room.

RECYCLING

Cleaning out mom's house, I thought at first I'd try to save us, the many framed and matted us. I could, or would, find spots in my own house for the under-glass mishmash of us and the dregs of our history. Someone getting a diploma, someone a black eye. A fish. A Jedi sword. A war bond.

I stare back at the stares and wonder if my sister's sidelong smirk or my nephew's cast-down glance convey clues I missed years ago but will suddenly sense as today's twilight falls upon the late-breaking now.

But no. My eyes are tired. Too much sepia has made them ache. The black and whites just seem covert and mean.

Then finally, frames and all, I just gather us up and toss us. Having once loomed so large in one another's eyes, we barely fill half the recycling bin. A girl on Santa's lap; a boy in a back row in first grade; same boy on a sled. His mother/my sister; his granny/my mother; and then me. As I chuck in the small weight of our brief histories, somebody blinks a last time into a cold blue wall. Stacks of us. Clutter of us. We came. We went. In a flurry our gazes cross and weave and drop.

FUNNY HA-HA?

"There're things you are not," my sister said once, "and one of them is a Southern Belle."

Funny, the context has fuzzed out; I can't recall to what she was replying.

For months after she was gone, I kept wondering if what she'd done was an act others had foreseen as likely and only we, her family, had not? Was everyone else whispering to each other, *Duh, we saw* that *coming; she had "deliberate overdose" written all over her?*

Duh was a word that woke me and sent me into cold rooms in the wee hours. *Duh* was how I sat there, my hands clenched, a woodpecker drilling its one word through the middle of my shivering core.

Her boy was ten. He stood between my mother and me, his damp palms in ours, as the coffin went down. She'd been ill, we told him. All we'd ever told him or ever would. All we'd tell anyone, really.

Funny then how the boy's bowing out was like a staged reproduction of his mother's. Funny that the boy was so funny about the remake. Did he know how funny? Did he think it was funny?

WHAT OH WHAT TO WEAR

Not the ladybug earrings and certainly not the teal heels even though
they travel well. It is not an eyeliner sort of day, not a blush afternoon.
Didn't the fangs I once wore make her lurch back—witch sister? which
sister? . . . the one hovering in a black sheath? or the one with lips
stitched into pink forgetfulness?

Consider the mourners more. Give them the unctuousness of grey
hose, the cliché of black pumps. In this sweater I too much resemble
her. Should I save the pennies from her loafers to cover my own eyes?
Which of us does that damn?

The silk scarf isn't purple enough to rewind the pleas, the please.
Won't these pearls let me tell the one who says, "Oh she looks like
she's sleeping so peacefully," *No, no she does not. I have seen her sleeping
and she never looked like that, with each of the hands I once clung to now
clinging only to one another . . . from here through the rest of time.*

SHORTLY BEFORE THE FIRST TIME MY NEPHEW WENT TO JAIL

For a short time his last semester had floated towards him and then away. As he watched the enormity retreat, a spring wind hurled the finally-dry fall leaves at his face.

I called him inside. I stood as a heavy beam he'd have to pass to get through the doorway.

"You're always high, your teacher says. She's not passing you."

He'd turned 18. I was as good as dead to him.

He ducked by and punched the teacher's note out of my hands. The wind slammed the door on us.

We had two more weeks. Two more. Before the sirens. Before the deep relief inside my dark ache.

Driven off, he hadn't even glanced back at the dead one who'd outlive him.

THE OTHER CHEEK TURNS

Today I finally take my dead sister's cowgirl boots to the Salvation Army, where the collection woman oohs and ahs, and I reply, *I know, I know. I wish I could wear them but they're way too big,* and then I buy a flowerpot, and as I'm leaving, I'm offered a prayer which is already flying through me before I can escape it. The stranger had my soul at heart. *Amen, Amen,* I kept saying, trying to hurry her along, my flowerpot growing heavier as its emptiness deepened.

MISTER ED SAYS, "HELLO, EARTH GIRLS"

Ed says, "I'm only on earth for a short time with a gold flick for you and you, and hey, come for a live chat; stay for the apple.

"You, girlies, idle hands are *not* the devil's workshop—quit listening to your mother!

"Sweetie pies, you don't know the trouble I've seen. And really, there's no such thing as If-The-Shoe-Fits. The shoe, she always fits."

Little Hope, Little Sarah Belle

**Step into
the Scott
Enchanted Forest
. . . and relax**

*By the time you learn
the wildflowers' names
you will be
safely under them.*

Scott . . . paper products throughout the New York World's Fair

X.

SCOTT ✕ MAKES IT ALL BETTER

BEAUTY IN THE BRONZE AGE

(Musée d'Unterlinden, Colmar, France)

Of the skeletal remains under glass, the arm bones were intact but
the fingers missing. Perforated saucer of skull. Thick bronze bracelets
gone green. No, the person had been *a man*, I translated and so ad-
vised the German woman who'd told her husband *a girl*.

The woman frowned, then glared down at the bejeweled slivers of
wrist bones as if they could, or should, explain themselves.

The man had also worn four necklaces and the same sort of hoop earrings my sister liked, which made me smile and try to picture exactly
which small ones we'd made her wear in her casket since there'd been
that huge church around us and the only allowable grandeur drifted
down from a nail through the lord's feet.

COULD HAVE SHOULD HAVE

On the prone one's cold forehead, my warm hand. Pressing down. To make what's real there enter me.

To stand close to where that stone cliff-face deepens our last moment, an icy fault cracks in the mind, and the lacy edge of a wild-flowered meadow recedes in the far distance.

No doubt an account like this is best received as a glancing breeze. A blink and a by-your-leave. Such is the way I tap and touch and depart again: brief cool drafts as someone flips the page.

SOME BOY WITH A FOOTBALL

The slow snow first and then the hard snow with left and right men shoveling, cars swerving, stalling, spinning out, and drip by drip the icicle daggers sharpening, waiting to descend as we women lug logs up the porch steps and the dogs slink off, shivering, tails between their legs.

And "Good God," a granddaddy shouts at some boy—with no ear-muffs!—holding out a football, offering it to our great frigidity. A once-human hand, a bare beige hand, extending its offering.

And behind the hand, the young face watches us work in the world. Against the world. Some boy. I guess he was mine for a while.

THIS SHIT CAME BEFORE THAT SHIT

Mom told me she'd paid your dealer with Great Granny's china. She said she'd peeked out a window and watched the dealer stare into the box she'd left on her porch stoop, his mouth forming the words *Un-Be-Liev-Able* over and over.

This was back in your heroin days, which were, thankfully, short-lived—since you'd been put on a plane and flown out to me. I had a place in Kansas. My first teaching job. In a college now defunct. This was before your baby. Before even the plan of a baby.

Standing in my Kansas kitchen, you told me I lived in a "godforsaken hellhole." And once, when I'd been away, you went out, coatless, on a cold rainy night to a neighbor's farm, knocked, and asked if they had any cough medicine. Mentioned you were my sister.

The next day they called and said you'd been shivering and coughing and "wearing only a nightgown and robe!" They gave you all they had, even your favorite: the cherry stuff with the codeine. All of it.

You took all of it.

I just sighed, thinking, Well, no wonder she's still asleep.

But when I hung up, I went to check to be sure. Sure that you were: Just. Asleep. Your chest rose and fell so quietly. The day before when I'd asked you about the needle scabs between your toes, you'd said you were all done with that. Said you wanted to live.

Standing in the doorway, I recalled more of Mom's tale about the dealer, how by the time he'd bent and picked up the box of china, he was laughing. Then she'd reminded me about those dishes. Purportedly they'd belonged to her grandmother who'd come over on a ship from England in the 1880s. This was a short part of a long story I'd heard for many years, a story which back then I still believed.

THE GOOD CHEST

I can't tell her, I say, stepping into my husband's arms and leaning my forehead on his chest.

"Tell who what?

Tell my sister—

"—your sister's dead."

I know but—

"Tell her what?

Tell her Mom's bonkers now and can't remember her.

"You don't have to"—he pulls me closer—"tell her."

I tap my head against his chest as if beating it against a wall. The old wall. The good chest.

"You don't, you don't," he says in time with his pulse.

I do, I do, I say in time with mine.

ASSISTED LIVING

I sit with the oldsters outside on the last warm afternoon—as it turns out—of the year. We watch the shiny cars and loud trucks whizz by. My mother waves and says she thinks she knows him, or her, or them, and Betty says he or she comes by here all the time asking for food. Then Margaret sighs and says she misses driving. Jim says he misses pets. Dot says she misses nicknames. Since all the lawn chairs are occupied, I sit in mom's walker, eyes closed, imagining myself as a shadow beneath the huge maple, the wind striating the shadow's shape, leafing it out, nicking its edges, cars running over it. Mom says she misses her bike. Jim misses his boat. Betty misses the creek at the end of her road.

WE MUSE ON HOW MISTER ED CAME BY HIS STRANGE ABILITIES

A spell's been put on him? Something from the human world he ate! I suggest.

But how odd that Wilbur has never inquired. *Perhaps Ed is divine,* I pose. I'm eleven. In a couple of months I'll pass my confirmation class and, wearing Nani's gloves, receive a white Bible that'll leer, fifty years later, from atop its tall private shelf in a dusty cellar.

My six-year-old sister scrunches her nose, meaning *no.* Not divine. "Could he have a man inside him?" she asks.

A live man?

She shrugs. Already we converse along different wavelengths. She's the microwave to my infrared.

Maybe most horses can talk, *but Ed's the only one to try.*

She shakes her head and gives the horse in her *Mister Ed World* book the wild turquoise mane he'll always toss around in my mind. Then she lets go a whinny that's nothing like Ed's. Hers is the cry of a tiny foal.

XI.

. . . *visit the home*

that talks!

The silver beneath these streets has
vanished—every last vein, one pulse
at a time. The walls of empty shafts
shake themselves, and at any second

    your life could drop
        through a cellar chute
            into the narrow channels
                of other folks' history,

where once there seemed good reasons
for bad debts, for mud and guns and grease.
Reasons your name stayed like sour milk
in everyone's mouth . . . high upstairs.

Twelve minutes of happy adventure.
Don't miss it.

IN MOM'S OXY DREAM

She's saying goodbye to a husband, but which one she's not sure. She waves a hand and the husband waves a hand, and at first there's a valley then gradually a whole town between the hands. Tall buildings. A river, *our* river. Many bridges. She shows me the wave: a gesture of so-long-to-everything.

Predawn, she walks through the house trying to find a way back to the dream, to touch the hand, hers to his, and see again the valley within the town that she assures me was *no* dream. "Quite real," she says. "Nothing fake about it." She holds up her palm. We both peer into it: the busy tracks in, the meandering tracks out.

SHELF LIFE

Blah, blah—I just go on making books. For a while each one is a large thing in my mind; then slowly each shrinks to a small dot beside its brethren dots . . . all in a tidy row on their own white shelf.

Once the dots and I had intense communications: complex jigs and jags in a lexicon that felt chewy, hearty. These days the dots keep their own counsel. I blink at them as I pass. My blinks say, *Hi there, So long.*

But it's okay. We get each other. Especially in a certain hour of dusk when the dots glow red, downright bloody from the window's reflected sunset, I sense their kind regards: *Hello. Carry on. We're all fine here.*

CARRYING ON

You're dead, I used to tell my sister in the dreams. Lately I just flash her a wan smile. Even asleep, I feel the corners of my mouth curve up.

She goes on and on. She has much to say about everything. "Mom's silver serving set. Why is it so black? Why can't you get around to polishing it? Why are you so busy?"

I'm not, I say.

"I know! But you think you are."

I feel my smile droop.

"And Nani's irritated. You promised you'd iron those pillowcases. And don't say you're writing. Nobody gives a shit about that. This dream is better than any poem. It's better than a cruise to Mexico. Better so much better than . . . ."

What's best, I've learned, is to let her have her say. Soon enough she'll shrug, then go smoke out back, the way she always did, on my porch stoop.

WHAT GOES AROUND

The dishes come back. In the same box. To the same spot on Mom's front porch. She calls me crying. She thinks the dealer's sending her a message. But what? The dishes are in pieces. Nani's dishes. What does it *mean?*

By this time my sister's started nursing school. Trying. Again. Another stab at a regular life.

"You'll make it." "God never gives us more than we can bear." Hearing such drivel, she'd laugh, turn on her heel, and walk away.

Thirty years later, I laugh when I open the box Mom's saved. Saved, for no reason she can recall. We've been cleaning out her garage since, at 75, she's moving, marrying a third husband. He's 85. They'll have 15 good earth years together.

I'm taking the box, I tell her.

"Fine. I don't ever want to see that stuff again." She pats the lid like a dog's head.

Okay. I nod. *Don't worry.*

But I break my word. My mother sets her glass of iced tea on a mosaic tabletop I've recently made from those very dishes, all broken, all shards. We're sitting out back on my deck. It's been two years since my stepdad's death (at 100!). She tells me I've done a good job on the tabletop, and it's clear as she glances at the bits of plates and saucers—*pique-assiette*, the term for this tile work—she remembers nothing about them.

The pieces of pieces. My hands pressed chips into grout. I sanded and smoothed and sealed.

I worked on my back deck, where in the evenings the marmots climbed up from the river to see what all the racket had been about.

They leapt about, gleeful, happily nibbling a petunia and giving not the tiniest shit about the useless human and her useless human rubble.

No doubt one day soon they'll pee on my table.

Let them.

Days beneath the sun are good. For no reason I recall. A harder hammering here. Less grout there. More smashing! More smashing! Nani once ate off this edge of a china-rose. Once this crack hurt us. Nani's hands in the suds, my hands in the sanding. In France an old man built a whole house this way, then went and lived inside it.

HOLE FOR THE HATCHET

A pink flower had grazed the empty pot on my porch, blinked, and blown on by. Jar of baby food on a shelf one day, in the garbage the next. That child had made me open myself, close myself, and hate myself—sometimes all in a single minute.

Years after he dies, I go out and dig a hole for the hatchet but the hole just keeps shrinking, even as the hatchet enlarges. And *why* has it suddenly attached itself to my ankle? *Ow*—Criminy!—how does that thing stay so sharp?

Ow was the cry an owl made over our pathetic antics by that hole as the hatchet blade went on muttering to my freshly dug dirt, *Shut up! Take nothing—Nothing—from this woman hacking away at the very ground beneath her.*

HATCH IT!

Hatch this! I shout up and offer the circling magpies a black onyx egg. *You'll like it! I know how you gruesome squawkers love the dead.*

Sit on it.

Forever and a day.

Egg with a royal, albeit inaudible, pulse within.

Just a little something.

From our nest to yours.

A LOZENGE AT DUSK

My cursive cursing all the way, I wrote all morning in italics since that's how my hand went today. Come dusk, I fold the page—fold after fold after fold!—into a tiny square. Here then, I tell my tongue, suck on this.

ORDINARY EXCHANGE

Mom: "How long have you known me?"

Me: I say my age.

Mom: "How long have I known you?"

Me: I say my age again.

Mom: "That's a long time."

Me: I smile and nod.

Mom: "Do you think you'll remember me after I'm gone?"

Me: "Yes. As long as I can remember anything."

Mom: "I'll remember you too. After I'm gone."

COOLING IT IN THE CLARK FORK

Behind me it is tomorrow, and I am set down between two mountains today, my sandals staring patiently sunward.

Haven't I crossed here once already? Was it even in *this* life?

Or had I been dipped, headfirst, then quickly lifted?

Ah, to lie back on the riverbank, musing on a heel withstanding the flow of time.

But which one? And how?

Always the consequent task: to reconstitute oneself, get up, hike a mile, smack a horsefly, and drive on. So much more of the West to go.

MISTER ED ALOFT

Forget the circus, Mister Ed wants to join space! To be NASA's first horse in orbit. But dagnabbit, he's too fat.

Vowing to *work* off the pounds, he allows himself to be hitched to a plow. My sister and I scoot closer to the screen. Harnessed Ed fills our den with woe.

The plow, he reports, is the weight of the world.

Next it's Plow-Ed vs. an enormous tree root, a small man, and the man's snarling whip.

In dreamspace, Ed's capsule is a giant pill with a svelte horse inside. He orbits, majestically high above two kids who've just rolled on their backs so as not to see the ad that follows: delicate diamond-studded fingers holding Out Out Out the stupid earth's stupid offering: a mentholated freshness, the puff we should take of springtime.

"IT'S A SMALL WORLD,"
sing animated figures,
but it's also
THE VAST MAYBE
and you're supposed to
have something to say
about it. Your job's wires
cross with the Bolsheviks'.

Fire-wands and
the parallax beams
your stubby pencil throws out.

Souls in the crosshairs, and No,
comrades, not of the sort
lost in shipwrecks.

NOT SAYING BOO

My sister was in the hospital, her ankles draining, something I could see in my mind's eye, although she was two thousand miles due west. I was teaching then in Illinois, and one day I brought a visiting poet-friend to my place in the country. He wanted to see my newly born lambs.

As we walked slowly across the yard towards the pasture, he'd been saying he thought the best poems had less to do with the business of society and more to do with the condition of one's soul. I was a young woman when he said this. It stopped me. He smiled into the sun and broke off a tall stalk of grass. Neither of us had, as yet, messed up our lives as badly as we would. Although my family debacles were another decade away, his were just months off.

I opened the gate and we stepped through and were immediately met for inspection by the oldest ewe. Me she found boring, but *he* was interesting. He was new. He caressed her black snout—something she'd never allowed me.

The lambs gamboled about. Soon I'd have to band their tails and, using the Double Crush Emasculator tool, neuter the males—chores I didn't mention to my friend. Nor did I say how most talk of souls made my gut go tight, rattled and lengthened my already restless nights.

I didn't say boo about any of that. Instead I reached out and grabbed the shoot of grass my friend had been about to put in his mouth. "Don't eat that," I said. "We're in a pasture."

SO THE VAST MAY BE

Scarlet Runner Beans. Back in May someone must have planted them around the gazebo for the shade they'd be right then—mid-September and huge blooms fluttering around a blurry-eyed me who looks up, startled by so much red.

Behind me, inside the old folks home where my sister had worked, the memorial service for her had just ended: hymn-singing and testimonials from grey-hairs in wheelchairs, from mouths trying to talk around dentures that no longer fit.

She had been a kind nurse, one person said. She liked to tease, said another, or tell a bawdy joke.

During the recessional, while some ancient bald head bent over the Chopin, the dark bass keys' clatter sounded almost discordant against the sweet higher notes. As a girl, my sister had played this same sonata, rocking a little over one part or another, while I watched, perched on a stair, annoyed because the song had gone on too long and too loud and disturbed my reading. But seeing her small head dip and bow, watching it nod down into the Polish man's pain, I'd finally shrugged and walked back upstairs into the twenty years she and I had left . . . before this quaint quiet inside a respite of blazing flowers.

YES & NO

Once she'd asked me, "Think things will get better in another twenty years?"

And twenty-some years later I answer the empty teacup that's her stand-in: *Well yes, but also no. Yes: the organic produce is great. So's the coffee. Pot is legal. We have gay weddings, which are ten times* more *fabulous than straight ones. OMG, I love a woman in a tux! You would too, you would, you so would.*

And no. Christ, the hurricanes. The fires out west all around and closing in, and now the water's going too. Just as we thought. It feels like the edge of apocalypse.

And no . . . since your boy didn't make it. But yes, he had a high old time like you, like you, very you.

And yes because I have a bicycle with a battery! Extra power for a little assist up the wonderful paved trail, which runs where the old tracks ran and is new and quite nice except for the pervert who leaps out and jiggles his dick in your face. But yeah, you know me, I just whizz on by.

SUPER CUTS

She buttons me into a silky blue cape, and I smile when she tells me her name. "America." *Good name,* I say. But she's already busy scrutinizing my skull, turning it like a doll's. Then she suggests "the hairdo the head needs."

Ok, let's do 'er, I say and she nods and begins the painstaking snip-snip-snip. Bits of my hair rise in her fingers, and fall. I close my eyes and let America do her work. America is a genius, I think. I love how between snips her hand fluffs the bits of hair back together with the others.

Slowly, under her touch, her rhythm of lift and drop, of chop and fluff, I fall into a trance.

Then "Hey, how's she look?" America suddenly asks me.

We both stare into the mirror at my head as it tips slightly, considering itself. Then it nods, and so does she.

I pay and go and drive into sleet. Through jarring potholes. Thinking of America with a stranger's head in her hands, an unknown anyone deeply taking in a good hour's dream so as to ward off a suddenly unfamiliar road, cold and black as the barrel of a gun.

SISTER ZERO

Morphined up, my sister had been saying she'd wake next as a swim-noodle—"ha ha!"—to "buoy us."

See? See? Across the distant waves? That soft sister o stretched out out   out   into a numeral 1. *Something* . . . something about the codes.

The eyes blink.   Think!   All *possible* codes.

Dark rumors on dark winds had herded us inside the buoys. We float-wonders. Treading. Treading near the wide loud mouth of the coldest deepest blue.

> For all indented porpoises,

> > there bobbed no threat,

> > > no prize, no matter.

A WHINNY IS THE WAY

A ten-year-old sat close to Ed. Riveted, but confused. Wilbur, however dear-hearted, you are a pushover. A schemer, a dodo, a weakling, a teller of tales, a hearer of impossible voices.

The viewer gathers her yellow hair into a ponytail. Finally she's inferred the meaning of "hangover troubles." Also, it's okay that Wilbur's wife Carol walks all over him. See how he buffs away any angry residue with silliness and smooth talk, which consequently leads naturally to an All's-Well, punctuated by a quick kiss to seal the deal.

Ed's golden. Filled with finality. Let's hurry to the barn for the answer that we'll endorse: an animal solution to today's human fuckup.

Oh, how nice, there's a sleigh waiting! And ah, that's a sweet touch, those snow bells!

Everyone piles in; everyone trusts *someone,* surely *someone* knows the way. Ed sighs and pulls. He throws his gold mane. Oh bother. A harder tug and louder whinny—yes, that's the way, all day, to pull the sleigh.

CODICIL OF SELECTED EXCISIONS, CHAPTERS IX-XII

—tomorrow's another story. Is it? Is it really?

—Can the small person be jealous that someone else's life story gets its ending, while the small person's story just goes on to some unseeable endnote on the filthy jig-jaggedy continuum? This thought: as unfinished as fuck.

—the neighbors leaving the cemetery drove the dusk closer to the bright yellow backhoes, whose engines I felt sure were about to start up.

—she was high on the hill. There, gone. Now me. High on a hill.

—I drove by the prison, thinking the baby's in there. Her baby. My charge. Except for a small corner of the building, all the window lights went out at once. I tried to imagine the ensuing sounds—the calling, crying, cursing, or maybe . . . maybe a simple sudden quiet.

—I hated knowing all the languages of emergency. The banality of them. The blood red outline of the ciphers in space. The pitch of the screech. The sirens. So knowing. I can't. Even.

—all morning as I kept expecting the horse to appear at my window and tell me a knock-knock joke, the meadow rolled in instead. Ah, the rolling. The rolling is how a meadow most excels.

ACKNOWLEDGMENTS

Thanks to the editors of these journals for publishing portions of this book:

Agni: "He Wore a Badge," "Idiot," "Super Cuts," "In Charge of Nothing," and "Codicils of Selected Excisions."

The Bellingham Review: "Awaiting Developments," "We Roll Our Eyes," "The Attic's Not So Far," "In the Affirmative," and these collages: "However Dear the Price," "What You'll See at the Fair," and "Entertainment for Everyone."

Cincinnati Review: "Assisted Living" and "My Husband's Story."

Cleaver: "Boy with Football," "Brows," and "Vast Old Age."

Crazyhorse: "To Be Beautiful" (as "The Bronze Age"), "Ed: Strange Abilities," "Futurama," "Monitors of the Guestbook," "Her Life," "What the Hell Indeed," "Little Pomp," "Ed: Aeronautical," "More and Less," "Ed: FDR," "Live with It," "Binaries," "Panhandler," "Ed: Oats," and "Sky Story."

Denver Quarterly: "Ed Talks of Jonah and the Host."

Gettysburg Review: "Jonah Riding It Out," "What Oh What to Wear," "The Baby," "From Whatever House," "Yes and No," "Neck of the Woods," and "Funny Ha-ha?"

High Desert Journal: "Recycling," "This Shit Came Before That Shit," "Broken Ribs," "Tiny Tears," "I Ducked Out the Back Door," "What Goes Around," "Mixed Toxicities," "Trading Vehicles," "Hole for the Hatchet," and "Hatch It!"

Iowa Review: "Midway on the Continuum" (as "Five Years Later Talking About the Dead Woman") and "Dressing."

Minnesota Review: "Landerluden."

9th Letter: these collages: "Wonder Rotunda," "The Vast Maybe," "Time Capsule Components," "Dream Big Pucker," "To the Moon and Beyond," "Autopsy Report in Progressland," "The Equitable Life," "Tectonic Face," and "High Upstairs."

North American Review: "Mister Ed Aloft," "Home with Me," "My Sister's Spiel," and "Sister Zero."

Ploughshares: " Mister Ed Claims Jonah First Considered Skedaddling."

Post Road: "Shortly Before the First Time My Nephew Went to Jail," "Dang It," and "Ordinary Exchange."

Southern Poetry Review: "What State Are We In?"

Stringtown: "Would Have Could Have Should Have."

West Branch: "I Step Off, Late," "Big Os," "Fault Vs. Vault," "Lozenge," "The Other Cheek Turns," "Vault Vs. Fault," "How High ARE You?" "Making it to Vast Old Age, So What," "With Ribbons Untied," "Finis," "On Two Green Noodles," and "My Report Card."

This book was set in FF Scala and FF Scala Sans, designed by Martin Majoor and published in 1991. Originally commissioned by the Vredenburg concert hall in Utrecht, Netherlands, Scala's name is an allusion to the famous opera house in Milan. Similar to Eric Gill's Joanna, Scala was inspired by the designs of Pierre Simon Fournier in the mid-eighteenth century, but also bears the influence of Renaissance humanist typefaces.

This book was designed by Shannon Carter, Ian Creeger, and Gregory Wolfe. It was published in hardcover, paperback, and electronic formats by Slant Books, Seattle, Washington.

Cover photograph by Vitolda Klein on Unsplash.

CPSIA information can be obtained
at www.ICGtesting.com
Printed in the USA
BVHW041154231022
650028BV00001B/91

9 781639 821174